'That's not cyber bullying, those are your GCSE results'

THE BEST OF
MATT
2015

MATTHEW PRITCHETT

studied at St Martin's School of Art in London and first saw himself published in the *New Statesman* during one of its rare lapses from high seriousness. He has been the *Daily Telegraph*'s front-page pocket cartoonist since 1988. In 1995, 1996, 1999, 2005, 2009 and 2013 he was the winner of the Cartoon Arts Trust Award and in 1991, 2004 and 2006 he was 'What the Papers Say' Cartoonist of the Year. In 1996, 1998, 2000, 2008 and 2009 he was the *UK Press Gazette* Cartoonist of the Year and in 2015 he was awarded the Journalist's Charity Award. In 2002 he received an MBE.

Own your favourite Matt cartoons. Browse the full range of Matt cartoons and buy online at www.telegraph.co.uk/photographs or call 020 7931 2076.

'Aaaaarrrrggghhhhh'

The Daily Telegraph

THE BEST OF

2015

An Orion Paperback

First published in Great Britain in 2015 by Orion Books
A division of the Orion Publishing Group Ltd
Carmelite House
50 Victoria Embankment
London
EC4Y 0DZ

A Hachette UK Company

10 9 8 7 6 5 4 3 2 1

© 2015 Telegraph Media Group Limited

A CIP catalogue record for this book is available from the British Library.

ISBN: 978 1 4091 4834 0

Printed in the UK by CPI Group (UK) Ltd, Croydon, CR0 4YY

The Orion Publishing Group's policy is to use papers that are natural,
renewable and recyclable products and made from wood grown in
sustainable forests. The logging and manufacturing processes are
expected to conform to the environmental regulations of the country of
origin.

www.orionbooks.co.uk

'I think I've invented the migrant crisis'

THE BEST OF
MATT
2015

'If the election has just begun, what have I been ignoring since Christmas?'

'It's not Shakespeare, but this is the third election manifesto I've written today'

'Did you mention immigration to the Labour candidate?'

Kitchens enter the debate

General Election

'Yes, I do want to discuss our relationship, but only if the Greens, UKIP, SNP, DUP and Plaid Cymru are included'

'We reached a compromise. Cameron, Clegg and Miliband will present Top Gear'

Talks about talks

'Under Labour, solar eclipses would be less dark and the NHS would be exempted'

General Election

'It all sounds much too French for my liking'

'I'm a Don't Know. But
I'm a VERY passionate,
pumped-up Don't Know'

'Tories took credit for the
sunshine, SNP said it did
nothing for Scotland, UKIP
said it was un-British and
Labour asked how it was
being funded'

Polls suggest unpredictable result

General Election

Polls – they were wrong

'Oh no! Just as I learned to stop calling him Ed – or do I mean David?'

'We'll always have our student loans to remember them by'

Scottish Referendum

'The problem with
independence is that there
are too many unknowns in it'

'I've noticed a slightly
intimidating and bullying
atmosphere creeping
into this battle'

'I don't mind the midges,
but we're plagued by
Westminster politicians'

'Nicola Sturgeon'

Businesses fear Yes vote

'In this one Mel Gibson
wins extra tax and welfare
powers for Scotland'

'HEY! I've just had
quadruplets. Is anyone
paying attention?'

Meanwhile . . .

Greek Crisis

'To show solidarity with the Greek people we won't be paying this bill'

Greek Crisis

'My divorce was like
Grexit – but less amicable
and more expensive'

'I have a bad feeling
about this'

'They've run out of pencils'

'And if you missed any of the Greek crisis, it will be repeated in a few months' time'

Immigration

'As with immigration numbers, this is an ambition, not a target'

'I found the immigration minister hiding in the back of that lorry. He was trying to flee to Calais'

Numbers up

'How was your school trip to Calais?'

Immigration

'A migrant got in our car, but after we sang Wheels On The Bus and played I-spy he leapt out again'

'If they've come to claim benefits, they're going to get a nasty surprise'

'That's fine, but next Christmas we're going to them'

'You can't ALL be osteopaths!'

'Football has ruined money'

FIFA

Heatwave

Alcohol

'My wife and I do our own
Ice Bucket Challenge
most evenings'

'Sometimes I drink the
following day's allowance.
I'm up to January 4th 2034'

'We didn't bring a bottle.
We got you these tablets for
mild alcoholism instead'

'It's important to have two
alcohol-free days a week.
We employ a chap in the
village to do ours'

Economy

'This could be the day I'm forced out of the pound'

'I've been working at the Treasury. I can't say too much, but it involves George Osborne, a hat and me'

'The Joneses are knocking down their extension. We should knock ours down too'

'Great news! HS2 is going through our garden – our property will be worthless'

Defence

'In the event of war, we can parachute into enemy territory and dig a well'

'The defence cuts have freed up these magnificent starter homes'

'Wait! If you're taking me to A&E I'd like to rent out my house'

'The good news is that since you've been here that vase has become an antique'

'Look! There's that nice couple we met waiting for a train after Christmas'

'It's a disused railway station. They say some nights you can still hear the wailing of the season ticket buyers'

'There are lots of price
cuts around and I don't
want to pass them
on to our customers'

'Tonight in Wolf Hall,
Henry VIII switches to his
sixth energy provider'

Low Inflation

'I remember when you could buy a pint, have a haircut and go to the cinema for exactly what it costs now'

'I bought you next year's card now, while low inflation is keeping prices down'

'This is serious – we must rig
the Bank Fines Mechanism'

Libor scandal

'I'll be late home. There are
8,000 leaving parties'

Charlie Hebdo

'Be careful, they might have pens'

'The British jihadists are
the ones wearing socks
under their sandals'

'I wanted to become a
jihadist, but round here the
internet's too slow and
there's no mobile reception'

Three Parent Babies

'One of my three parents
really likes you'

'Son, there's something your
mother and I have to tell you
about three-parent babies'

'Wake up. Our duck down
duvet just sneezed'

Bird flu

'Your luggage had a
temperature, so we lost it'

Ebola

Celebs in Trouble

'My horse is involved
in a slight fracas'

'In the final episode,
the Dowager Countess is
told she's missed dinner
and a fracas ensues'

Clarkson

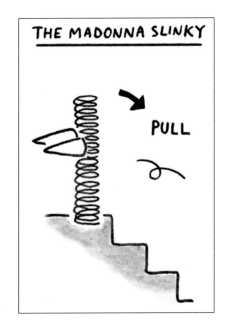

Madonna's fall

Celebs in Trouble

'I'm doing the Knowledge.
We have to learn all
David Mellor's job titles,
awards and honours'

'I know I'm the family's
taxi driver, but you can't call
me a stupid, sweaty s***'

Mellor's taxi rant

'Someone has leaked a
nude oil painting of our
déjeuner sur l' herbe'

'WE'VE FLOWN
INTO AN iCLOUD'

Images hacked

Russian Aggression

'We must be nearly back
over the UK; I keep seeing
Russian bombers'

'The Russian bomber
that just flew overhead
curdled our clotted cream'

I wandered lonely as a cloud
That floats on high o'er vales
and hills,
When all at once I saw a crowd,
A host, of bloody fracking drills

'We're fracking for worms'

Women Bishops

'It's a woman bishop, it can move any way it wants'

'I'm against female bishops, I believe a woman's place is on the front line'

'Are we nearly there yet?'

'Would you take him
in part exchange?'

Kevin Pietersen

'No, not enlightenment –
I'm seeking naked women'

'Are you trying to tell me
that you want to go
mountaineering?'

Tory Budget

'I don't have to pay my Merry Men the living wage, do I?'

'He was hit by a champagne cork, Sarge'

'I was 35 when I decided I
didn't want to have children,
but it was too late'

'He's had a wonderful day'

Seven Day NHS

'This is a little delicate but, now you'll be working at weekends, could I take over your golf club membership?'

'I was disappointed to see you in church last Sunday, Doctor'

MAGNA CARTA
800 YEARS

'I don't care if she is the
Queen, she's subject to
parking restrictions like
everyone else'

PRINCESS CHARLOTTE'S
FIRST SELFIE

And finally . . .

'They've got subsidy blight'

'We shouldn't get sentimental about them; they carry so much disease'

Heatwave

Air rage

And finally . . .

'Today is SATURDAY? Well,
I didn't see that coming'

'I threw my hat in the ring
and Paddy Ashdown ate it'

Election night pledge

'I went online and paid
someone to write
a fake review'

'We're not doing a nativity.
We're doing a play
about the dangers of
middle-class drinking'

And finally . . .

Pluto photos

Weasel photos

'I think it's
fizzy drink o'clock'

'On holiday he took a packet
of salted nuts from the hotel
mini-bar without paying'

And finally . . .

GOLDILOCKS GIVES A LIFT
TO THE THREE BEARS

'The inside lane is too slow, the outside lane is too fast, but the middle lane is just right'

'So that flashing light on the dashboard wasn't a warning about the global economy'

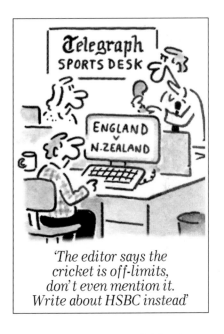

HSBC coverage criticised

And finally . . .

And finally . . .

'That's lovely, darling.
I'd like to hear it again
in 35 years' time'

'I'm a Scottish MP, can I
be excluded from this?'

English votes for English laws

'I didn't have a sixpence for
the Christmas pudding,
so I put in 7,000 roubles'

Currency collapse

And finally . . .

'Now have a lollipop – it's
probably more effective
at preventing flu'

'It's such a relief to ditch the
Human Rights Court and
get back to common sense'

'When the oil price crashed,
we switched to dairy farming'

Dairy farming problems

'Maybe it was a mistake to
re-introduce beavers'

And finally . . .

'Taste the dog's dinner to check it's not been poisoned'

Crufts scandal

'The tax disc holder was the only thing keeping your car together'

'Listen, I've loved spending time with you, but I'm flying back to Gatwick and the chances of us seeing each other again are almost nil ...'

'Speeding? This isn't my driverless car, it's my wife's driverless car'

And finally . . .

Feminist T-shirts

Celebrity plastic surgery

'Go away! I'm watching the Bake Off final'

'I'm so depressed. I've been eating only veg and I'm back up to 65 tons'

BIGGEST EVER DINOSAUR FOUND

Dentist shoots lion

'After being released, he ordered three books from Amazon'

'The time? Yes, it's ten minutes past my battery dying'

And finally . . .

And finally . . .

'The school run is so much
easier with a drone'

'You didn't call, you didn't
text. We've been worried sick'

'With this App you
can find the nearest
MPs for hire in your area'

'I haven't had my flu jab yet,
so I've come here to
avoid human contact'

And finally . . .

'I wish people wouldn't dump
Tesco chairmen in the pond'

'They say their records
indicate that we may have
been involved in an accident
that wasn't our fault'

Nuisance calls

'I don't care if it is
Harrison Ford. You have
to be proposed by three
members to crash land here'

'I'm just saying, we could
catch the World Cup final
and THEN go to Bethlehem'

Qatar World Cup

And finally . . .

'How heterosexual are your fairy cakes?'

Gay wedding cake

*Roses are red
Champagne is bubbly
Have a wonderful day
I'll be at the rugby*